Hidden Depths

Guided/Group Reading Notes

Blue Band

Contents

Introduction 2

Guided/Group reading notes

1. Character story: *Operation Shipwreck*
   by Anthony McGowan 12

2. Character story: *Toxic!*
   by Jan Burchett and Sara Vogler 18

3. Character non-fiction: *Beneath the Ice*
   by Martyn Beardsley 24

4. Variety story: *Journey to the Centre of the Earth*
   by Paul Shipton 30

5. Variety non-fiction: *Exploring the Deep*
   by Chloe Rhodes 36

OXFORD

Introduction

Reading progression in Year 5/Primary 6

By Year 5/Primary 6 the majority of children are developing into confident, capable readers. The focus is on continuing to build their enjoyment, reading fluency and their engagement with reading. Encouraging children to read widely in order to develop personal preferences, critical appreciation and comprehension is central to helping them become enthusiastic readers. Humour, adventure, suspense and identification with interesting characters and intriguing information texts all help create books children look forward to reading. They can sustain independent reading for extended periods of time but chapters and non-fiction spreads offer natural 'break points' for readers who may still find long texts challenging to read. They also create hooks to motivate the reader to want to read further.

Year 5/P6 children recognize most common words on sight. The texts at **blue band** include polysyllabic and more complex topic-based vocabulary. Explicit work on vocabulary continues to be important for improving both reading and writing. Introducing new vocabulary within meaningful contexts helps to extend children's vocabulary range. A wide range of vocabulary, sentence structures and verb tenses are used. Language play (puns, homophones, homonyms, codes, jokes, onomatopoeic words, etc.) can be found in the texts. Expressive, descriptive and figurative language and vocabulary help create moods and emotions.

In the fiction books, storylines are more complex, involving, for example, subplots or parallel settings. For example, in the **Hidden Depths** cluster, the character stories move between the safe location of NICE headquarters to various locations around the world.

The non-fiction books, too, are increasingly complex. They raise interesting discussion opportunities as well as providing a wealth of fascinating material. For example, the factual information about what lives beneath the sea gives some background to the character stories concerning the dangers of polluting the planet.

The non-fiction books offer examples of a wide range of genres. There are opportunities to compare and contrast different opinions and viewpoints and to evaluate situations and arguments. Texts may contain a balance of fact and opinion, and encouraging children to distinguish between these helps them respond critically. Factual information is presented in a range of formats.

Visual literacy is supported through the range of visual 'genres' used in the books, for example, comic strips, photo sequences and diagrammatic 'animations'. At blue band, the ratio of text to illustration is greater, but the illustrations continue to provide additional information and interest for the reader, including opportunities to compare and contrast visual information and source materials. Photos and illustrations add to the content and level of reading challenge, rather than simply supporting the text. Visualization comprehension strategies and activities that encourage the reader to reflect on the visual images are suggested in these *Guided/Group Reading Notes*.

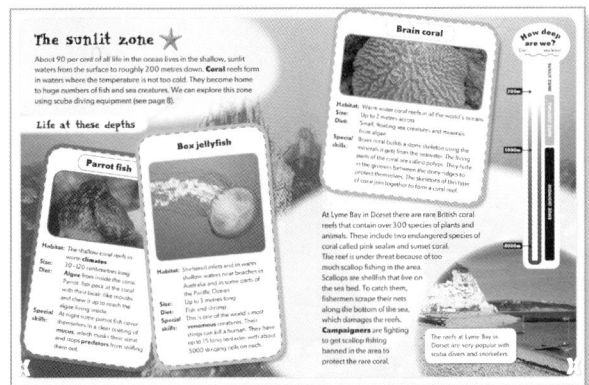

The character books

The character stories at blue band show the children working as a team for Dani Day, who has become senior scientist for the National Institute for the Conservation of Earth (NICE). The children's adventures take them all over the world. In some stories they also encounter, and have to outwit, a new villain – the Collector. The Collector has one goal – to own the biggest collection of snow globes in the world. Using advanced micro science, he shrinks and steals valuable objects. It is up to Team X to stop him. The Collector taunts the children with riddles and clues, and he also commands a new X-bot – the Master-bot. The children need ingenuity and creative thinking to get out of the tricky situations they find themselves in as they try to thwart the Collector. Luckily, they have a range of new micro-sized gadgets and X-crafts and the backup of Dani's scientific expertise to help them.

While looking for a missing shipwreck in the first character fiction book, *Operation Shipwreck*, the children realize that the Master-bot is involved. A rare mammal will be in danger if the ecosystem is disturbed, so Team X is sent to the Greek Islands to investigate. They work under pressure as a team to outwit the Collector and save the ecosystem.

In *Toxic!* Dani sends the children to an area of outstanding natural beauty in Canada that is being mysteriously destroyed. Team X use the Driller – an underground X-craft – and teamwork to solve the problem and have a terrifying encounter with a very strange creature on the way.

The character non-fiction book *Beneath the Ice* features Sir John Franklin, the Arctic explorer, and the attempts to find him.

Guided/Group reading

By Year 5/P6, guided/group reading sessions offer opportunities for children to read independently in a focused way and take part in group discussion to enhance understanding, personal response and an appreciation of the author's craft, rather than concentrating on rehearsing and applying reading cues – although there may be occasions when revisiting these is useful.

These *Guided/Group Reading Notes* provide support for each book in the cluster, along with suggestions for follow-up activities. Suggestions are given for three guided/group reading sessions for each book. However, at blue band, children may read much of the book independently and only undertake one or two guided reading sessions around the text. Although guided/group reading suggestions are given under each section of the notes, teachers will select which chapters/non-fiction sections they wish to use in reading sessions.

Children may record their thoughts, feelings and understanding of a book in a reading journal. A section on using reading journals is given in the *Teaching Handbook* for Year 5/P6.

Speaking, listening and drama

Talk continues to be crucial to learning. At Year 5/P6, children still need plenty of opportunities to express their ideas through talk and drama and to listen to and watch the ideas of others. These processes are important for building reading engagement, personal response and understanding, and for rehearsing some writing possibilities. Suggestions for speaking, listening and drama are provided for every book. Within these *Guided/Group Reading Notes* the speaking and listening activities are linked to the reading assessment focuses.

Building comprehension

Understanding what we have read is at the heart of reading.
To help readers become effective in comprehending a text these *Guided/Group Reading Notes* contain practical strategies to develop the following important aspects of comprehension:

- Previewing
- Predicting
- Activating and building prior knowledge
- Questioning
- Recalling
- Visualizing and other sensory responses
- Deducing, inferring and drawing conclusions
- Determining importance
- Synthesizing
- Empathizing
- Summarizing
- Personal response, including adopting a critical stance.

The research basis and rationale for focusing of these aspects of comprehension is given in the *Teaching Handbook* for Year 5/P6.

The Project X *Interactive* software for Years 5 and 6/P6 and 7 contains comprehension activities for every book. In addition, higher comprehension skills are developed through activities in the 'Explore' section.

Reading fluency

Reading fluency combines automatic word recognition, reading with pace and expression. Rereading, fluency and building comprehension are linked together in a complex interrelationship, where each supports the other. This is discussed more fully in the *Teaching Handbook* for Year 5/P6. Opportunities for reading aloud are important in building fluency and reading aloud to children provides models of expressive fluent reading. Suggestions for purposeful and enjoyable oral reading and rereading/re-listening activities are given in the follow-up activities to these *Guided/Group Reading Notes* and in the notes for parents on the inside back cover of each book.

The Project X *Interactive* software allows individuals or small groups of children to listen to the texts. Listening to stories being read, and hearing the text in the non-fiction books, is particularly effective with EAL children.

Building vocabulary

Explicit work on enriching vocabulary is important in building reading fluency and comprehension. By Year 5/P6 children have a familiar core vocabulary and reading is the most important means by which children encounter new vocabulary. However, further work needs to be undertaken if newly encountered written words are to become part of the child's vocabulary repertoire. Suggestions for vocabulary work are included in these notes. The vocabulary chart on pages 10–11 shows some of the ambitious vocabulary introduced in each book, along with vocabulary linked by meaning. Reusing new words orally or in their own writing helps these words become integrated into the child's working vocabulary. The chart also indicates those words that can be used to support a structured spelling programme.

Developing a thematic approach

Helping children make links in their learning supports their development as learners. All the books in this cluster have a focus on the theme of **Hidden Depths**. A chart showing the cross-curricular potential of this theme and further reading suggestions are given in the *Teaching Handbook* for Year 5/P6, along with a rationale for using thematic approaches. Some suggestions for cross-curricular activities are also given in these *Guided/Group Reading Notes*, in the follow-up suggestions for each book.

In guided/group reading sessions, you will also want to encourage children to make links between the books in the cluster. Grouping books in a cluster allows readers to make links between characters, events, actions and information across the books. This enables readers to gradually build complex understandings of characters and information, to give reasons why things happen and how characters may change and develop. It can help them to recognize cause and effect. It helps children reflect on the skill of determining importance, as a minor incident or detail in one book may prove to have greater significance when considered across several books.

Note that the books in this cluster can be read in any order.

In the **Hidden Depths** cluster, some of the suggested links that can be explored across the books include:

- working as a team **(Citizenship, PSHE)**
- learning about pollution and the delicate balance of the Earth's ecosystem on the land as well as in the sea **(Geography, Science, PSHE)**
- exploration and how it can be used to help save the planet. **(Science, PSHE)**

Reading into writing

The character books provide both models and inspiration to support children's writing. Brief suggestions for relevant, contextualized and interesting writing activities are given in the follow-up activities for each book. These include both short and longer writing opportunities. They cover a wide range of writing contexts so writers can develop an understanding of adapting their writing for different audiences and purposes.

The Project X *Interactive* software contains a 'Write and Respond' section for every book. This section contains a number of writing frames and activity sheets that pupils can write/type into directly, or print off, for extended writing. In addition, there is a collection of 'clip art' assets from the character books that children can use in their writing.

The section on Reading Journals in the *Teaching Handbook* for Year 5/P6 contains a wealth of suggested activities that can be used with any text. You may also wish to draw on these during guided/group reading sessions.

Selecting follow-up activities

These *Guided/Group Reading Notes* give many ideas for follow-up activities. Some of these can be completed within the reading session. Some are longer activities that will need to be worked on over time. You should select those activities that are most appropriate for your pupils. It is not expected that you would complete all the suggested activities.

Home/school reading

Books used in a guided/group reading session can also be used in home/school reading programmes.

Before a guided/group reading session, the child could:
- read the first chapter or section of the book
- read a related book from the cluster to build background knowledge.

Following a guided/group reading session, the child could:
- reread the book at home to build reading confidence and fluency
- read the next chapter in a longer book
- read a related book from the cluster.

Advice for parents on supporting their child in reading at home is provided on the inside back cover of individual books. There is further advice for teachers concerning home/school reading partnerships in the *Teaching Handbook* for Year 5/P6.

Assessment

During guided/group reading, teachers make ongoing reading assessments of individuals and of the group. Reading targets are indicated for each book and you should assess against these. Select just one or two targets at a time as the focus for the group. The same target can be appropriate for several literacy sessions or over several texts.

Speaking and listening targets and writing targets are also given for each book, as guided/group reading sessions support these other modes of communication. One possible speaking and listening target and one writing target are given, linked to the suggested follow-up activities. The many suggested oral and writing tasks give ample further opportunities for other aspects of speaking and listening and writing to be assessed.

Readers should be encouraged to self-assess and peer-assess against the target/s.

Further support for assessing pupils' progress is provided in the *Teaching Handbook* for Year 5/P6.

Continuous reading objectives and ongoing assessment

The following objective will be supported in *every* guided/group reading session and is therefore a continuous focus for attention and assessment (AF2/6). This objective is not repeated in full in each set of notes, but as you listen to individual children discussing their reading you should undertake ongoing assessment, against this objective.

- Reflect on reading habits and preferences and plan personal reading goals **8.1**

Further objectives are provided as a focus within the notes for each book, as appropriate, from these strands:

- Understanding and interpreting texts *(Strand 7)*
- Engaging with and responding to texts *(Strand 8)*.

Specific spelling objectives are not given with each book but some spelling and vocabulary building opportunities are indicated in the sessions.

Correlation to the specific objectives within the Scottish, Welsh and Northern Ireland curricula are provided in the *Teaching Handbook* for Year 5/P6.

Recording assessment

The assessment chart for the **Hidden Depths** cluster is provided in the *Teaching Handbook* for Year 5/P6.

Diagnostic assessment

If an individual child is failing to make good progress or he or she seems to have a specific problem with some aspect of reading you will want to undertake a more detailed assessment. In the *Teaching Handbook* for Year 5/P6 checklists for reading attitudes and behaviours are given to assist with this. There is also a running record sheet for Blue band, or you may wish to track back to the running record sheets for Grey band in the *Teaching Handbook* for Year 4/P5.

Vocabulary chart

At Year 5/P6, children should:

- read most words independently and automatically
- spell words containing unstressed vowels
- know and use less common prefixes and suffixes, such as *im-, ir-, -cian*
- group and classify words according to their spelling patterns and their meanings.

NB. Examples only are given in each category.

Operation Shipwreck	Less common prefixes/ suffixes	mis–: mischief con–: consequences, concentration dis–: disappearance
	Spelling pattern	Compound words: shipwreck, rucksack, seatbelt, corkscrewing, zigzagging, wireless, something pp: strapped, flipped, toppled, rippled
	Ambitious vocabulary	Mediterranean, desperately, shrunken, refuges, analysing, endangered, inquisitive, stabilize, spiralled, aquatic, mechanical
	Vocabulary linked by meaning	Historical vocabulary: archaeologist, ancient, Roman galley, British frigate, seventeenth century Venetian trading ship

Toxic!	Less common prefixes/ suffixes	in-: investigate dis-: disappeared anti-: anticlockwise il-: illegal
	Spelling pattern	ion: devastation, mission, communication
	Ambitious vocabulary	irritated, blackened, reluctantly, shimmered, slunk, furiously, eerie, crumpled, manoeuvred, accelerate, shuffling, tentacles, aggressively
	Vocabulary linked by meaning	Words related to the forest landscape: lush, foliage, wilted, withering, environmental, dense Words related to pollution: contaminated, pesticides, mutated, seeping
Beneath the Ice	Words containing unstressed vowels/ consonants	island, government
	Spelling pattern	ion: mission, region, navigation
	Ambitious vocabulary	unforgiving, ventured, experienced, conquer, necessary, underestimate, perseverance
	Vocabulary linked by meaning	Arctic expedition vocabulary: temperature, expedition, scientist, icebreaker, circumnavigated, abandoned, survived
Journey to the Centre of the Earth	Words containing unstressed vowels/ consonants	glimpse, climbing
	Spelling pattern	en: deafening, hardened, brightened, suddenly ion: determination, destination, rationed ious: furious, unconsciousness
	Ambitious vocabulary	incredible, gravely, communicate, flicker, hauled, interrupted, despair, amplified, trudged, cascaded
	Vocabulary linked by meaning	Prehistoric vocabulary: granite, dinosaurs, ichthyosaurus, plesiosaurus
Exploring the Deep	Less common prefixes/ suffixes	en-: enclosed, endangered
	Spelling pattern	ll: shellfish, scallop, snorkellers, shallow, colliding, propeller
	Ambitious vocabulary	fearsome, communicate, decibels, microscopic, photosynthesis
	Vocabulary linked by meaning	Scientific vocabulary: camouflage, photophores, temperature, oxygen, hydrothermal

Operation Shipwreck

BY ANTHONY MCGOWAN

About this book
Team X meet their old adversary the Collector again. He has sent his evil Master-bot to the Aegean Sea to steal the wreck of a sunken treasure ship. The ecosystem is in danger ... can Team X stop him?

Big themes: teamwork, leadership qualities, bravery, working under pressure

Writing genres: narrative, emails, character profile, fact files

You will need
- *Prediction and reflection grid* Photocopy Master 24, *Teaching Handbook* for Year 5/P6
- *Expedition* Photocopy Master 7, *Teaching Handbook* for Year 5/P6

	Literacy Framework objective	Target and assessment focus
Speaking, listening, group interaction, and drama	○ Perform a scripted scene making use of dramatic conventions **4.2**	○ We can perform a scene to show our feelings about the characters **AF3**
Reading	○ Compare different types of narrative and information texts and identify how they are structured **7.3**	○ We can recognize the language choices and structures of different types of text **AF4/5**
	○ Explore how writers use language for comic and dramatic effect **7.5**	○ We can recognize and discuss how the author makes the story dramatic **AF5/6**
Writing	○ Experiment with different narrative form and styles to write their own stories **9.2**	○ We can write a chapter in the form of a play script **AF1/2**

The following notes provide a structure for up to three guided/group reading sessions. They can be used flexibly; you can focus on all three sessions, two or one session. The rest of the book can be read independently by the children between sessions.

Select appropriate activities from the suggestions below depending on whether the children will read during the session or whether they have read prior to the session. In this instance you will skip the 'During reading' section, although, you may wish to include the 'As you read' activity as part of your discussion of what they have read independently. In Session 1, children will read Chapters 1–3. Prior to Session 2, ensure they have read Chapter 4 independently. In Session 2, they will read Chapter 5. Prior to Session 3, ensure they have read Chapter 6. In Session 3, they will read Chapters 7–8.

Session 1 (Chapters 1–3)

Before reading

To activate prior knowledge

- Discuss the title 'Operation Shipwreck'. Which type of organizations call their investigations and activities 'operations'? **(activating prior knowledge)**
- Look at the map on pages 4 and 5. Can the children locate the UK and other countries in Europe, and the Mediterranean Sea/Atlantic and Pacific Oceans? Can they link any current news stories to any place discussed? **(activating prior knowledge)**

To support engagement with the text and encourage prediction

- Read pages 2 and 3 to the children. Model fluent reading through the pace and expression of your reading.
- Working in pairs, ask the children to predict what sort of 'mischief and mayhem' the Collector might do in this book. They could use the *Prediction and reflection grid* Photocopy Master to record their thoughts. **(predicting)**
- Before children read independently, ask them to rehearse what they might do if they become stuck on a word or sentence. The range of possible strategies (such as rereading, reading on, using context, using phonic, syntactic and vocabulary knowledge) should be well established for most readers and only an occasional reminder should be necessary.

During reading

- Ask the children to read Chapters 1–3.
- Stress the importance of comprehension, reminding the children to stop and take action if they are failing to understand the text, e.g. by checking the meaning of a particular word or phrase, rereading more carefully, reading on to see if the meaning becomes clear, reading it aloud, discussing the passage with someone else, etc.
- As they read, ask them to spot how page 13 has been designed to reflect the non-fiction text type.

> **Assessment point**
>
> Listen to individual children reading and make ongoing assessments on their approaches to tackling new words, their reading fluency and their understanding of the text. AF1

After reading

Returning to the text

- Ask the children:
  - Where does the story take place? (**recall**)
  - Why was the Collector gazing thoughtfully at his globes? (**deducing and inferring**)
  - *Extension question:* Why is the monk seal in danger? (**drawing conclusions, synthesizing**)

The author's craft

- Discuss why the last two lines of Chapter 1 are so effective and ask why the author has used italics for '*now*'.
- Why has the author written such a short Chapter 3?

> **Assessment point**
>
> Can the children recognize the language choices and structures of different kinds of text? AF4/5

Building comprehension

- During a short guided writing session, demonstrate how to change the beginning of Chapter 2 from narrative into play script. Ask the children to work in pairs to complete the script of the chapter.
- The children can then perform the scene from their script, using gestures to reflect how the characters are feeling.

> **Assessment point**
>
> Can the children show their ideas and feelings about the characters in the story clearly? AF3

- Prior to Session 2, ensure the children have read Chapter 4 independently.

Session 2 (Chapter 5)

Before reading

To review previously read text
- Ask the children to briefly recap the story to date. (**recall**)

To encourage prediction
- How might the Green Dart help the characters to stop the Master-bot from turning the wreck into a snow globe? Ask the children to fill in their *Prediction and reflection grid*. (**predicting**)
- Before children read independently, ask them to rehearse what to do if they become stuck on a word or sentence.

During reading

- Ask the children to read Chapter 5.
- Stress the importance of comprehension, reminding the children to stop and take action if they are failing to understand the text.
- As they read, ask them to think about how each member of Team X reacts to the situation.

> **Assessment point**
>
> Listen to individual children reading and make ongoing assessments on their reading fluency. AF1

After reading

Returning to the text
- Ask the children:
  o What was stirring up the sediment on the sea floor? (**recall, inferring**)
  o Why did Tiger grin on page 30? (**inferring**)
  o Ant begins to 'fiddle' with the control panel on page 31. What does that tell the reader about his capabilities? (**inferring**)

- *Extension question:* How did each character react during the battle with the X-bots? Use evidence from the text. (**inferring and drawing conclusions, synthesizing**)

The author's craft

- Tiger says 'Uh, oh' on page 28 when he is faced with all the X5 guards. Ask the children to discuss with a partner why the author has deliberately chosen such an understated phrase. What does this tell them about Tiger? (**adopting a critical stance, inferring**)
- *Extension activity:* On page 31, the author shows the reader how Max and Tiger were feeling without telling us that they were frightened (e.g. 'heart hammered'). Ask the children to discuss this with their partner and then write how Ant and Cat might be feeling at this point, using similar techniques.

> **Assessment point**
>
> Can the children explain to their partner, with examples from the text, the effect of the author's language choices? **AF4/5**

- Prior to Session 3, ensure the children have read Chapter 6 independently.

Session 3 (Chapters 7–8)

Before reading

To encourage prediction

- Ask the children to predict what will happen in the rest of the story. (**personal response, predicting**)
- Before children read independently, ask them to rehearse what to do if they become stuck on a word or sentence.

During reading

- Ask the children to read Chapters 7–8.
- Stress the importance of comprehension, reminding the children to stop and take action if they are failing to understand the text.
- As they read, ask them to reflect on their response to the whole story. (**personal response**)

🔍 After reading

Returning to the text
- In pairs, ask the children to discuss what they thought of the story. They could also complete their *Prediction and reflection grid* Photocopy Master if they started one. (**personal response, including adopting a critical stance**)

The author's craft
- How does the author build excitement in the last chapter? How do the illustrations help the reader? (**deducing, inferring, determining importance, adopting a critical stance**)

> **Assessment point**
> Can the children explain how the author makes the story dramatic? AF5/6

Building comprehension
- Ask the children to complete a storyboard, summarizing the final chapter in twelve frames. (**visualizing, summarizing, determining importance**)
- Ask them to use this to turn a chapter into a play script, drawing on the conventions of play script explored in Session 1.

> **Peer assessment point**
> Ask the children to assess each other's script, taking into account the conventions of the genre. AF1/2

Follow-up activities

Writing activities
- Choose one member of Team X and write a character profile, using the one on page 3 as a model. (**short writing task**)
- Use the *Expedition* Photocopy Master to advertise a visit to a Mediterranean shipwreck. (**short writing task**)
- Write a confidential email explaining how Team X was able to stop the Collector this time. (**longer writing task**)

Cross-curricular and thematic opportunities
- Look at underwater images in Google Earth to find out what the sea really looks like. (**Geography, ICT**)
- Design a snow globe using Photoshop. (**Art and design**)
- Compose an underwater musical scene with parts representing the tranquillity of the water, the fish, the wreck, the turtle (p.24) as Team X arrived. Use graphic notation to record the composition and perform it. (**Music**)

Toxic!

BY JAN BURCHETT AND SARA VOGLER

About this book

Team X is sent to investigate what is causing the death of a beautiful area of Canadian forest. What they find is astonishing.

Big themes: teamwork, leadership qualities, ecology

Writing genres: narrative, blog, email, fact files

You will need

- Globe, atlases
- *Canadian National Parks* Photocopy Master 8, *Teaching Handbook* for Year 5/P6
- *Vocabulary bookmark* Photocopy Master 18, *Teaching Handbook* for Year 5/P6
- *What are they thinking, feeling, saying?* Photocopy Master 27, *Teaching Handbook* for Year 5/P6
- NICE 'Mission Accomplished' report Photocopy Master 2, *Teaching Handbook* for Year 5/P6

	Literacy Framework objective	Target and assessment focus
Speaking, listening, group interaction and drama	○ Present a spoken argument, sequencing points logically, defending views with evidence and making use of persuasive language **1.2**	○ We can argue a case persuasively **AF2/3**
Reading	○ Make notes on and use evidence from across a text to explain events or ideas **7.1** ○ Explore how writers use language for comic and dramatic effect **7.5**	○ We can track ideas and information across a story **AF2** ○ We can recognize and discuss how the authors make the story dramatic **AF5/6**
Writing	○ Experiment with different narrative form and styles to write their own stories **9.2**	○ We can write a story in the first person **AF1/2**

The following notes provide a structure for up to three guided/group reading sessions. They can be used flexibly; you can focus on all three sessions, two or one session. The rest of the book can be read independently by the children between sessions.

Select appropriate activities from the suggestions below depending on whether the children will read during the session or whether they have read prior to the session. In this instance you will skip the 'During reading' section, although, you may wish to include the 'As you read' activity as part of your discussion of what they have read independently. In Session 1, children will read Chapters 1–2. Prior to Session 2, ensure they have read Chapter 3 independently. In Session 2, they will read Chapter 4. Prior to Session 3, ensure they have read Chapters 5–6. In Session 3, they will read Chapters 7–8.

Session 1 (Chapters 1–2)

Before reading

To activate prior knowledge and encourage reflection

- Look at pages 2–5 together. Check that the children understand the aim of NICE (protection of the planet and the precious things in it).
- Using atlases or a globe, locate Canada and Cape Breton. You could also refer to the *Canadian National Parks* Photocopy Master which could be completed later.
- Before children read independently, ask them to rehearse what they might do if they become stuck on a word or sentence. The range of possible strategies (such as rereading, reading on, using context, using phonic, syntactic and vocabulary knowledge) should be well established for most readers and only an occasional reminder should be necessary.

During reading

- Ask the children to read Chapters 1 and 2.
- Stress the importance of comprehension, reminding the children to stop and take action if they are failing to understand the text, e.g. by checking the meaning of a particular word or phrase, rereading more carefully, reading on to see if the meaning becomes clear, reading it aloud, discussing the passage with someone else, etc.

- As they read, ask them to note any new or unusual words and record these on their *Vocabulary bookmark* Photocopy Master for discussion later.

> **Assessment point**
>
> Listen to individual children reading and make ongoing assessments on their approaches to tackling new words, their reading fluency and their understanding of the text. **AF1**

After reading

Returning to the text

- Ask the children:
    - In her blog, what does Mandy say she has found? (**recall**)
    - Why was Tiger late for the meeting? (**recall**)
    - Why did Dani warn the team that what they might find could be nasty? (**inferring**)
    - *Extension question:* Why is Tiger so negative? (**empathizing, inferring and drawing conclusions**)

The author's craft

- Look at the last three paragraphs on page 15. Identify all the words and phrases which bring the action to life. (**adopting a critical stance**)

> **Assessment point**
>
> Can the children recognize and discuss how the authors build the drama? **AF5/6**

Building comprehension

- Ask the children to role play the scene on page 12 and freeze frame where Cat gazes round at the devastation of the forest. Ask each character what they are thinking and feeling at this point. How could they persuade Tiger that something needs to be done? (**empathizing, personal response, adopting a critical stance**)

- Ask the children to complete the *What are they thinking, feeling, saying?* Photocopy Master for one of the characters. (**empathizing, adopting a critical stance**)

> **Assessment point**
>
> Can the children argue about how the forest is being destroyed by pollution and persuade Tiger that something needs to be done? **AF2/3**

Building vocabulary

- Share the words the children have recorded on their vocabulary bookmarks. Look at them in context and check they understand the meaning.
- Ask them to highlight all the ecological vocabulary.
- Prior to Session 2, ensure the children have read Chapter 3 independently.

Session 2 (Chapter 4)

Before reading

To review previously read text
- Ask the children to briefly recap the story to date. (**recall**)

To encourage prediction
- Look at page 23, and ask them to predict what sort of creature might be in the tunnel. (**predicting**)
- Before children read independently, ask them to rehearse what they could do if they become stuck on a word or sentence.

During reading

- Ask the children to read Chapter 4.
- Stress the importance of comprehension, reminding the children to stop and take action if they are failing to understand the text.
- As they read, ask them to notice the different functions of the Driller.
- Ask them to note any new or unusual words and record them on their bookmarks.

> **Assessment point**
>
> Listen to individual children reading and make ongoing assessments on their approaches to tackling new words, their reading fluency and their understanding of the text. AF1

After reading

Returning to the text
- Ask the children:
  - What was the animal? What is its most distinguishing feature and what is it used for? (**recall**)
  - What was wrong with the animal and how had this happened? (**recall, deducing, inferring and drawing conclusions**)
  - What does a skull and crossbones usually represent? What does this make the reader think? (**activating prior knowledge, inferring**)

The author's craft

Extension activity: Challenge the children to find all the hints the vocabulary gives as to what the creature might be, i.e. something not alien (e.g. *pawed*). (**inferring, deducing and drawing conclusions**)

- How is the tension created at the end of Chapter 4? How could children use this technique in their own writing? (**adopting a critical stance**)

> **Assessment point**
> Can the children explain how the authors build the drama? AF5/6

Building vocabulary
- Share the words the children recorded on their bookmarks. Look at them in context and check they understand their meanings.
- Prior to Session 3, ensure the children have read Chapters 5–6 independently.

Session 3 (Chapters 7–8)

Before reading

To review previously read text and encourage prediction
- Ask the children to discuss the story so far. How do the authors make the adventure exciting? (**recall, personal response, including adopting a critical stance**)
- What do they predict will happen next? (**predicting**)

To support engagement with the text and reading fluency
- Read pages 45–48 aloud. Model the excitement and tension in the prose and the different voices for each character and their feelings. Ask the children which techniques you used to bring the story to life.
- Before children read independently, ask them to rehearse what they could do if they become stuck on a word or sentence.

During reading

- Ask the children to read Chapters 7 and 8.
- Stress the importance of comprehension, reminding the children to stop and take action if they are failing to understand the text.
- As they read, ask them to reflect on their response to the whole story. (**personal response**)

> **Assessment point**
> Listen to individual children reading and make ongoing assessments on their reading fluency. AF1

After reading

Returning to the text
- In pairs, ask the children to discuss what they thought of the story. Which bits did they particularly like or dislike? (**personal response, including adopting a critical stance**)

Building comprehension
- Ask the children to complete a storyboard, summarizing the whole story in twelve frames. (**visualizing, summarizing, determining importance**)
- Ask them to skim the book, highlighting examples of Tiger's character through his reactions, then write the story from his point of view.

> **Assessment point**
> Can the children track ideas and information across the book? AF2

> **Peer assessment point**
> Ask the children to assess each other's writing, checking it has been written in the first person. AF1/2

Follow-up activities

Writing activities
- Reread page 39 and write a poem about being in this dramatic situation. (**short writing task**)
- Write Twitter entries throughout the day (maximum of 140 characters per entry). (**short writing task**)
- Write the end of mission report that Dani will file in NICE's records on the *NICE 'Mission Accomplished' report* Photocopy Master. (**longer writing task**)

Cross-curricular and thematic opportunities
- Devise a multimedia storyboard to create an animated version of the action. (**Art and design, ICT**)
- Research Cape Breton and other parks in Canada using the *Canadian National Parks* Photocopy Master. (**Geography**)
- Use a digital camera to produce a TV advert to persuade people to visit Cape Breton. (**ICT, Music**)

Beneath the Ice

BY MARTYN BEARDSLEY

About this book

Explorers have been searching for ways to cross the Arctic Ocean for thousands of years. This book highlights one adventurer – Sir John Franklin – and the extreme conditions he and his team had to face.

Big themes: exploration, survival in harsh conditions

Writing genres: non-chronological report, recount, explanation, instructions

You will need

- Globe, atlases
- *Vocabulary word map* Photocopy Master 19, *Teaching Handbook* for Year 5/P6
- *Life in the Arctic* Photocopy Master 9, *Teaching Handbook* for Year 5/P6

	Literacy Framework objective	Target and assessment focus
Speaking, listening, group interaction and drama	○ Use and explore different question types and different ways words are used, including in formal and informal contexts **1.3**	○ We can ask a range of questions **AF2/3**
Reading	○ Make notes on and use evidence from across a text to explain events or ideas **7.1** ○ Compare different types of narrative and information texts and identify how they are structured **7.3** ○ Distinguish between everyday use of words and their subject-specific use **7.4**	○ We can track information across a book **AF2** ○ We can identify the features of different text types and understand how this relates to their audience and purpose **AF4/6** ○ We can explain and comment on specific words and their uses **AF5**
Writing	○ Create multi-layered texts, including use of hyperlinks and linked web pages **9.5**	○ We can create an ICT text about Arctic exploration **AF1/2**

The following notes provide a structure for up to three guided/ group reading sessions. They can be used flexibly; you can focus on all three sessions, two or one session. The rest of the book can be read independently by the children between sessions.

Select appropriate activities from the suggestions below depending on whether the children will read during the session or whether they have read prior to the session. In this instance you will skip the 'During reading' section, although, you may wish to include the 'As you read' activity as part of your discussion of what they have read independently. In Session 1, children will read pages 2–7. In Session 2, they will read pages 8–17. Prior to Session 3, ensure they have read pages 18–23 independently. In Session 3, they will read pages 24–30.

Session 1 (pages 2–7)

Before reading

To activate prior knowledge and encourage prediction

- Look at the front cover and discuss the title. What could be 'Beneath the Ice'? Remind the children that the Arctic is frozen ice.
  (predicting, activating prior knowledge)

To support engagement with the text

- Read pages 2–5 together. Discuss the maps and use a globe to help explain the North-West Passage.
- Before children read independently, ask them to rehearse what they might do if they become stuck on a word or sentence. The range of possible strategies (such as rereading, reading on, using context, using phonic, syntactic and vocabulary knowledge) should be well established for most readers and only an occasional reminder should be necessary.

During reading

- Ask the children to reread pages 2–5 and then to the end of page 7 independently.

- Stress the importance of comprehension, reminding the children to stop and take action if they are failing to understand the text, e.g. by checking the meaning of a particular word or phrase, rereading more carefully, reading on to see if the meaning becomes clear, reading it aloud, discussing the passage with someone else, etc.
- As they read, ask them to note words on the theme of ice and the cold.

> **Assessment point**
> Listen to individual children reading and make ongoing assessments on their approaches to tackling new words, their reading fluency and their understanding of the text. **AF1**

After reading

Returning to the text
- Explain the difference between different question types: recall (answer is found easily in the text), inference (a clue to the answer is in the text) and synthesis (make connections, predict, draw conclusions).
- In pairs, ask the children to devise one question of each type to ask the group about the sections they have just read. (**questioning**)

> **Assessment point**
> Can the children ask a range of questions? **AF2/3**

The author's craft
- Look at pages 2–3 and ask the children to identify the features of a recount text: orientation (scene-setting opening); events (recount of events as they occurred); reorientation (a closing statement with elaboration).

> **Assessment point**
> Can the children identify the features of the text type and understand how it relates to the audience and purpose? **AF4/6**

Building vocabulary
- In pairs, ask the children to find and discuss the use of the themed vocabulary they identified earlier. Emphasize that details are needed in this genre to bring incidents alive.
- Complete the *Vocabulary word map* Photocopy Master.

> **Assessment point**
> Can the children explain and comment on specific words and their uses? **AF5**

Building comprehension
- Ask the children to comment on what they have read so far (content, features, layout, maps, etc). (**personal response**)

Session 2 (pages 8–17)

Before reading

To review previously read text/preview new text
- Ask the children to share any information they remember from the Session 1. (**recall**)
- Quickly skim through pages 8–17 to get an overview of their contents. (**previewing**)
- Before children read independently, ask them to rehearse what they could do if they become stuck on a word or sentence.

During reading

- Ask the children to read pages 8–17 independently, then go back and reread the sections that most interest them.
- Stress the importance of comprehension. Remind the children to be aware of whether they understand what they are reading and to stop and take action if they are failing to understand.
- As they read, ask them to think about which sections they have found most interesting and why. They could make brief notes in their reading journals. (**personal response**)

> **Assessment point**
> Listen to individual children reading and make ongoing assessments on their approaches to tackling new words, their reading fluency and their understanding of the text. AF1

After reading

Returning to the text
- Ask the children to talk about some of the sections/facts that interested them.
- Pair up the children who selected the same sections and ask them to devise questions for each other as they did in Session 1, taking turns to ask and answer the questions. (**questioning**)

> **Assessment point**
> Can the children ask a range of questions? AF2/3

The author's craft

- Look at 'How to make pemmican' on page 15. Identify the structural and language features of an instructional text (goal, materials, sequenced steps, use of imperative verbs).
- Ask the children to write a 'How to prepare for an expedition to the Arctic' instructional text using the survival facts on page 13.

> **Assessment point**
>
> Can the children identify the features of the text type and understand how it relates to the audience and purpose? AF4/6

- Prior to Session 2, ensure the children have read pages 18–23 independently.

Session 3 (pages 24–30)

Before reading

> **Peer assessment point**
>
> Ask the children to assess each other's writing, identifying whether they have used the features of the genre. AF4/6

To review previously read text

- Ask the children to tell you any fact from their independent reading. (recall)
- Before children read independently, ask them to rehearse what they might do if they become stuck on a word or sentence.

During reading

- Ask the children to read pages 24–30. They should be prepared to give an oral summary of one section.
- Stress the importance of comprehension, remind the children to stop and take action if they are failing to understand.

> **Assessment point**
>
> Listen to individual children reading and make ongoing assessments on their approaches to tackling new words, their reading fluency and their understanding of the text. AF1

After reading

Returning to the text/Building comprehension

- Ask each child to give a brief oral summary of their chosen section. (recall, summarizing, determining importance)
- As they talk, model making brief summary notes, adding page numbers and key points.

- In pairs, ask the children to make notes from the book in order to recount one of the expeditions or rescue missions described. Children should be prepared to retell the adventure using the notes, adding techniques such as exaggeration for effect and humour.

> **Assessment point**
>
> Can the children track information and ideas throughout the book and present their retelling in an engaging way? **AF2**

The author's craft
- Read and discuss the letter on page 22. Identify the features of letter writing.

Follow-up activities

Writing activities
- Ask the children to use their notes to develop an ICT-based report on Arctic exploration, adding hyperlinks to visual material, e.g. maps. (**longer writing task**)
- In pairs, discuss a way to rescue Franklin, and write a letter outlining the idea. Use the letter on page 22 of *Beneath the Ice* as a model. (**short writing task**)
- Write a recipe for a favourite food to take on an expedition. (**short writing task**)

Other literacy activities
- Draw a timeline showing all the expeditions to search for the North-West Passage from the Vikings to the present day.

Cross-curricular and thematic opportunities.
- Look at the timeline on pages 8 and 9. Develop a class timeline over a term alongside photographs of activities. (**History, PSHE**)
- Measure the maximum and minimum temperatures over a period of time and plot them on graphs. (**Science, Maths**)
- Compare and contrast desert and Arctic conditions and survival in each. (**Geography, Science**)
- Using the *Life in the Arctic* Photocopy Master, research how animals are adapted to the harsh conditions. (**Science**)
- Research icebreaker ships and explain their design and use. (**DT**)

Journey to the Centre of the Earth

BY PAUL SHIPTON

About this book

This is an adaptation of Jules Verne's story of the same name which was originally published in 1864. It is a fantasy adventure story in which the characters find themselves in a variety of exciting situations and meet some unexpected dangers, such as dinosaurs.

Big themes: code breaking, teamwork, bravery, determination

Writing genres: author notes, journal writing, first person narrative, fantasy and adventure, author interview

You will need

- *What are they thinking, feeling, saying?* Photocopy Master 27, *Teaching Handbook* for Year 5/P6
- *Story planning frame* Photocopy Master 14, *Teaching Handbook* for Year 5/P6
- *Victorian inventions* Photocopy Master 10, *Teaching Handbook* for Year 5/P6

	Literacy Framework objective	**Target and assessment focus**
Speaking, listening, group interaction and drama	○ Reflect on how working in role helps to explore complex issues **4.1**	○ We can use role play to explore ideas, texts and issues **AF2/3**
Reading	○ Explore how writers use language for dramatic effect **7.5** ○ Compare the usefulness of techniques such as visualization, prediction and empathy in exploring the meaning of texts **8.2**	○ We can recognize and discuss how the author makes the story dramatic **AF5/6** ○ We can use a range of strategies to explore the characters and meaning of a text **AF2/3**
Writing	○ Experiment with different narrative form and styles to write their own stories **9.2**	○ We can write a story in the form of diary entries **AF1/2**

The following notes provide a structure for up to three guided/group reading sessions. They can be used flexibly; you can focus on all three sessions, two or one session. The rest of the book can be read independently by the children between sessions.

Select appropriate activities from the suggestions below depending on whether the children will read during the session or whether they have read prior to the session. In this instance you will skip the 'During reading' section, although, you may wish to include the 'As you read' activity as part of your discussion of what they have read independently. In Session 1, children will read Chapters 1–6. Prior to Session 2, ensure they have read Chapters 7–10 independently. In Session 2, they will read Chapters 11–15. Prior to Session 3, ensure they have read Chapters 16–18. In Session 3, they will read Chapters 19–24.

Session 1 (Chapters 1–6)

Before reading

To activate prior knowledge and encourage reflection/prediction
- Discuss the title 'Journey to the Centre of the Earth.' Have the children seen or heard of the film of the same name? What kind of narrative can we expect? **(activating prior knowledge, predicting)**

To support engagement with the text
- Read the notes on page 2 to the children. Why would the girl Graüben have stayed at home in a Victorian story? **(inferring)**
- Before children read independently, ask them to rehearse what they might do if they become stuck on a word or sentence. The range of possible strategies (such as rereading, reading on, using context, using phonic, syntactic and vocabulary knowledge) should be well established for most readers and only an occasional reminder should be necessary.

During reading

- Ask the children to read Chapters 1–6.
- Stress the importance of comprehension, reminding the children to stop and take action if they are failing to understand the text, e.g. by checking the meaning of a particular word or phrase, rereading more carefully, reading on to see if the meaning becomes clear, reading it aloud, discussing the passage with someone else, etc.

- As they read, ask them to look out for clues about the personalities of Axel, the Professor and Graüben.

> **Assessment point**
>
> Listen to individual children reading and make ongoing assessments on their approaches to tackling new words, their reading fluency and their understanding of the text. **AF1**

After reading

Returning to the text

- Ask the children:
  - Where is Axel at the start of the story? (**inferring**)
  - Referring to the text, how do you know that Axel is worried by the adventure? (**deducing, inferring and drawing conclusions, synthesizing**)
  - How does Graüben feel about being left behind? (**empathizing**)

The author's craft

- *Extension question:* Why does the author start his story near the end of the action with Axel writing his journal? How does this affect you as a reader? (**inferring, personal response**)
- How is the suspense built up at the end of Chapter 6? Has the reader been given enough clues to predict who the figure might be? (**synthesizing**)

> **Assessment point**
>
> Can the children explain how the author builds suspense? **AF5/6**

Building comprehension

- Role play Chapters 3–5. Freeze frame the action at the point when the Professor says 'I can' (p.9). Ask the children to show how their character is feeling, then ask them to say how they are feeling. (**personal response, including adopting a critical response, empathizing**)

> **Assessment point**
>
> Can the children discuss how role play has helped them understand the thoughts and feelings of the characters? **AF2/3**

- Ask the children to complete the grid on the *What are they thinking, feeling, saying?* Photocopy Master for one of the characters at that point in the story. (**adopting a critical stance, empathizing**)
- Prior to Session 2, ensure the children have read Chapters 7–10 independently.

Session 2 (Chapters 11–15)

Before reading

To review previously read text

- Ask the children to briefly recap the story so far. Did they guess who the hooded figure was? (**recall**)
- Before children read independently, ask them to rehearse what they might do if they become stuck on a word or sentence.

During reading

- Ask the children to read Chapters 11–15.
- Stress the importance of comprehension, reminding the children to stop and take action if they are failing to understand the text.
- As they read, ask them to look for evidence that Axel seems to be more worried than any other character. (**inferring and drawing conclusions**)

> **Assessment point**
>
> Listen to individual children reading and make ongoing assessments on their understanding of the text. AF1

After reading

Returning to the text

- Ask the children:
  - What does the phrase 'all grinning like schoolchildren' on page 25 say about how the characters were feeling? (**empathizing, inferring**)
- *Extension question:* Where did the stream lead them to? (**recall**)

The author's craft

- On page 33, the author writes about the fish, 'It was a fascinating scientific discovery … and soon a tasty meal!' What does this expression add to the creation of the scene? Can the children explain the humour and the contrast between the two parts of the sentence? How could they use this type of expression in their own writing?

> **Assessment point**
>
> Can the children explain how the author's language adds to the drama of the story? AF5/6

- Focus on other expressions the author has used in the story. Explain the use of the simile 'as unbending as rock' on page 17. What insight does it give about Graüben's character?
- What expressions does the author use on page 21 to show how Axel is feeling as he looks down into the crater?
- Prior to Session 3, ensure the children have read Chapters 16–18 independently.

Session 3 (Chapters 19–24)

Before reading

To encourage prediction
- Ask the children to predict what will happen in the next few chapters. (**predicting**)
- Before reading independently, ask them to rehearse what they might do if they become stuck on a word or sentence.

During reading

- Ask the children to read Chapters 19–24.
- Stress the importance of comprehension, reminding the children to stop and take action if they are failing to understand the text.
- As they read, ask them to mentally note how the characters managed to get back up to the earth's surface.

Assessment point

Listen to individual children reading and make ongoing assessments on their reading fluency. AF1

After reading

Returning to the text
- Ask the children to explain how the group returned to the earth's surface. (**recall**)
- *Extension activity:* Ask the children to discuss in pairs whether they think the narrative is believable or not and to support their views. (**synthesizing, personal response, including adopting a critical stance**)

Building comprehension

- Ask the children to think about the situations Axel was in. Draw an emotions graph to show the significant changes in Axel's emotions in the pages they have just read and discussed. (**empathizing, determining importance**)

> **Assessment point**
> Can the children explain how visualizing a character helps them to think about the character's emotions? AF2/3

The author's craft

- In pairs, ask the children to find words and phrases to describe the heat of the volcano on pages 57 and 58. How do they help the reader to visualize the scene? (**visualizing**)
- Ask the children to imagine that they have a laptop which works deep at the centre of the earth. Ask them to write a Twitter entry (maximum of 140 characters) for each day for a small part of the adventure.

> **Assessment point**
> Can the children write about an adventure in the form of diary entries? AF1/2

Follow-up activities

Writing activities

- Write a short account, in the first person, of an adventure currently taking place in the news. (**short writing task**)
- Jules Verne wrote other adventure stories. Write a modern adventure story using all the technology we have available today. Use the *Story planning frame* Photocopy Master to help. (**longer writing task**)

Other literacy activities

- Turn the story into a play script and enact it. (**drama**)

Cross-curricular and thematic opportunities

- Research volcanoes and their position in the world. Locate Sicily, Stromboli and Iceland. (**Geography**)
- Research Victorian inventions using the *Victorian inventions* Photocopy Master. (**History**)
- Imagine you are organizing an expedition. Discuss the different types of personalities and skills it would be useful to have in your team. Are there some kinds of people who might be a burden on the expedition? (**PSHE**)

Exploring the Deep

BY CHLOE RHODES

About this book
What's beneath the waves? This books details what can be found deep in the oceans and how explorers and scientists have reached the depths.

Big themes: diving and underwater exploration, ocean creatures and features

Writing genres: non-chronological report, recount, explanation

You will need
- Globe, atlases
- *KWL* Photocopy Master 16, *Teaching Handbook* for Year 5/P6

	Literacy Framework objective	Target and assessment focus
Speaking, listening, group interaction and drama	○ Use and explore different question types and different ways words are used, including in formal and informal contexts **1.3**	○ We can ask a range of questions **AF2/3**
Reading	○ Make notes on and use evidence from across a text to explain events or ideas **7.1** ○ Compare different types of narrative and information texts and identify how they are structured **7.3**	○ We can track information across a book **AF2** ○ We can identify the features of different text types and understand how this relates to their audience and purpose **AF4/6**
Writing	○ Create multi-layered texts, including use of hyperlinks and linked web pages **9.5**	○ We can create an ICT text about exploring the oceans which is appropriate to the reader and purpose **AF1/2**

The following notes provide a structure for up to three guided/group reading sessions. They can be used flexibly; you can focus on all three sessions, two or one session. The rest of the book can be read independently by the children between sessions. You may, however, decide that it is not necessary for the children to read the whole book, or to read it sequentially.

Select appropriate activities from the suggestions below depending on whether the children will read during the session or whether they have read prior to the session. In this instance you will skip the 'During reading' section, although, you may wish to include the 'As you read' activity as part of your discussion of what they have read independently. In Session 1, children will read pages 2–15. In Session 2, they will read pages 16–23. In Session 3, they will read pages 24–30.

Session 1 (pages 2–15)

Before reading

To activate prior knowledge and encourage reflection

- Look at the front cover and discuss the title. Ask the children what they know about exploring the ocean and make brief notes on their *KWL* Photocopy Master under 'What I already know'. Looking at the contents page, and using the globe/atlases, ask them to work in pairs to discuss what they would like to know about oceans and seas. Make individual lists on the *KWL* sheet under 'What I would like to find out'. **(activating prior knowledge)**

To support engagement with the text

- Read pages 2–5 together. Discuss the zones and make sure the children understand the differences in depth.
- Before children read independently, ask them to rehearse what they might do if they become stuck on a word or sentence. The range of possible strategies (such as rereading, reading on, using context, using phonic, syntactic and vocabulary knowledge) should be well established for most readers and only an occasional reminder should be necessary.

During reading

- Ask the children to read on to the end of page 15.

- Stress the importance of comprehension, reminding the children to stop and take action if they are failing to understand the text, e.g. by checking the meaning of a particular word or phrase, rereading more carefully, reading on to see if the meaning becomes clear, reading it aloud, discussing the passage with someone else, etc.
- As they read, ask them to mentally note any answers to the questions on their *KWL* sheet.

> **Assessment point**
>
> Listen to individual children reading and make ongoing assessments on their approaches to tackling new words, their reading fluency and their understanding of the text. AF1

After reading

Returning to the text

- Discuss the differences between different question types: recall (answer is found easily in the text), inference (a clue to the answer is in the text) and synthesis (make connections, predict, draw conclusions).
- In pairs, ask the children to devise one question of each type about the sections they have just read to ask the group. (**questioning**)

> **Assessment point**
>
> Can the children ask a range of questions? AF2/3

The author's craft

- Look at the information cards on pages 6–7 and ask the children to identify the features of a non-chronological report: an opening title; a description of the phenomenon (including qualities, parts, habits, behaviour), third person, present tense.
- (W) Ask them to write an information card about themselves and share it with others.

> **Assessment point**
>
> Can the children identify the features of the text type and understand how this relates to the audience and purpose? AF4/6

Session 2 (pages 16–23)

Before reading

To review previously read text

- Ask the children to share one piece of information they have added to their *KWL* sheet.

- Before children read independently, ask them to rehearse what they might do if they become stuck on a word or sentence.

During reading

- Ask the children to read pages 16–23 independently, then to go back and reread the sections that most interest them.
- Stress the importance of comprehension, reminding the children to stop and take action if they are failing to understand.
- As they read, ask them to think about which sections they have found most interesting and why. (**personal response**)

> **Assessment point**
>
> Listen to individual children reading and make ongoing assessments on their approaches to tackling new words, their reading fluency and their understanding of the text. AF1

After reading

Returning to the text

- Ask the children to talk about some of the sections/facts that interested them.
- Pair up the children who selected the same sections and ask them to devise questions for each other, taking turns to ask and answer the questions. (**questioning**)

Building comprehension

- Ask the children to skim the book for animals, listing them under the various zones. (**summarizing**)

> **Assessment point**
>
> Can the children track information across the book? AF2

Session 3 (pages 24–30)

Before reading

To review previously read text

- Ask the children to tell you an interesting fact they have read. (**recall**)
- Before children read independently, ask them to rehearse what they might do if they become stuck on a word or sentence.

During reading

- Ask the children to read pages 24–30. They should be prepared to give an oral summary of one section.
- Stress the importance of comprehension, reminding the children to stop and take action if they are failing to understand the text.

> **Assessment point**
> Listen to individual children reading and make ongoing assessments on their reading fluency. AF1

After reading

Returning to the text
- Ask the children:
  - What is the midnight zone? (**recall**)
  - What is a hydrothermal vent? (**recall**)
  - Why is Mauna Kea in Hawaii called the world's highest mountain?

Building comprehension
- Ask the children to complete their *KWL* sheet and share their facts with a partner. (**summarizing, determining importance**)

Follow-up activities

Writing activities

- Choose one zone and create an online information pack for holiday makers, e.g. what to see and how to see it. Work in pairs to create a series of ICT pages that can be hyperlinked. (**longer writing task**)
- Research other famous shipwrecks and write information cards modelled on the ones on pages 10 and 11. (**short writing task**)
- Write a poem showing how it would feel and what someone would see whilst wearing a Jim Suit. (**short writing task**)

Cross-curricular and thematic opportunities

- Using the information on page 5 as a model, create a vertical axis which shows the highest mountain and the deepest trench. (**Maths, Geography**)
- Create a piece of music depicting a specific zone using tuned and untuned percussion. Record it. (**Music, ICT**)
- Draw food chains for each zone. (**Science**)